Back to Acts
How to start a home church

by Martin Holman

Worcester

Holman House Publishing

Intro: Jesus is Lord

For years people have been deconstructing their faith. I am no different. As a child, I grew tired of watching adults fight about whether or not women could wear pants or teenagers could listen to Christian music with drums, then attaching those rules to Scripture in some sort of epic false argument meant to control people. So I read Scripture and surprisingly read nothing about those things and began to ask what were the points that turned someone (specifically me) into a follower of Jesus.

Over time I realized anything could be broken down into something unnecessary, but what was necessary to become a Christian? What turned the alcoholic at the bar, the bully in the school, the addict on the streets, the shady, businessman, or the gossipy housewife into a fully devoted follower of Jesus? Or what took the uptight Baptist, the liberal Episcopalian, the crazy Pentecostal, the rocking Reformed, and the traditional Catholic and made them all one?

These questions haunt me to this day. In John 17, Jesus prayed that we would be one as he and the Father are one, and I see no evidence that his prayers are being answered in my lifetime or the foreseeable life of the church.

Of course this is tragic, but I believe I've put my finger on why it's happening. Most of the time when we think unity today, we think churches coming together with churches, which is another way of saying, organizations coming together with organizations. As you probably know, many churches are run like organizations. So churches attempt to come together.

At the dawn of the 2010's, Life.Church, a huge and generous technology savvy church brought thousands of churches together with their "One Prayer" series. Pastors uploaded their "One prayer" message to a unity website, and each church participating downloaded four different messages from four different pastors. It was an innovative series based on Jesus' call for unity.

The problem was it didn't build unity. Here's a secret you probably already know. Organizations don't want unity. Organizations want whatever purpose they are organized around. They attempt to achieve that purpose by cultivating certain practices that allow them to build up units of measurement they decide is important to them. For business organizations, that metric usually hinges around money. For churches, it's a hybrid measurement of people and money. When people and money become a commodity or measurement the church uses to figure out whether or not they are successful, the power of God is replaced with the power of business practice. There are ways to justify why this is necessary, but those ways always focus on the health of that particular organization.

The greater question all believers must face is how do we build unity at the church level and not just the individual level. How does First Baptist Church and St. Francis Episcopalian

Church integrate deep love into both their communication and praxis towards one another?

When we look into the early church in Acts and Paul's epistles, we begin to get an answer to these questions, and it starts with the size of the groups. Listen to this passage in Acts 2:

They devoted themselves to the apostles teaching and to fellowship, to the breaking of bread and to prayer. Everyone was a filled with awe at the many wonders and signs performed by the apostles. All the believers were together and had everything in common. They sold property and possessions to give to anyone who has need. Every day they continued to meet together in the temple courts. They broke bread in their homes and ate together with glad and sincere hearts, praising God and enjoying the favor of all the people. And the Lord added to their number daily those who were being saved.

This passage flows nicely and has been a rallying cry for churches in the modern age. But look at what Peter preaches in verse 36 that stimulates this response:

"Therefore let all Israel be assured of this: God has made this Jesus, whom you crucified, both Lord and Messiah." When the people heard this, they were cut to the heart and said to Peter and the other apostles, "Brothers, what shall we do?" Peter replied, "Repent and be baptized, every one of you, in the name of Jesus Christ for the forgiveness of your sins. And you will receive the gift of the Holy Spirit...."

It was clear the heartbeat of the church rested on Peter's proposition that God made Jesus, who was crucified, Lord and Messiah. N.T. Wright begins his book *Simply Good News* focusing on the historical drama of the great Roman civil war between Octavian vs Mark Antony and Cleopatra. In the end, Octavian won the war, and afterwards sent heralds across the Roman Empire declaring Caesar (Octavian) as Lord.

Now here were the apostles in the great Roman Empire subversively declaring the greatness of their Lord, Jesus the Messiah who would forever change history. Others had promised the same thing. Simon Bar Kokhba and a few other zealots claimed the Messianic title as their own and many even died for their belief, but most had no following and their names have been all but eclipsed from human history.

The apostles, however, staunchly claimed Jesus as Lord and maintained this as the bedrock of their faith. Throughout the last 2000 years, followers of Jesus repeat this mantra and it stands as the unifying cry of the body of Christ as a whole. No matter the denomination or the people group or the style of Christianity, a church or group cannot call themselves Christian if they don't profess that Jesus is their Lord.

The reason why this point is strong enough to introduce this book is that no church should be started or even maintained unless *Jesus is Lord* is believed and all ministries or programs launched from the church do so under this key principle.

There are a lot of good reasons to start a church, whether it be to see souls saved, bring people together to pray and fast, or be a light to your community. No reason, however, is more important than the idea that a group of people believe with their whole heart that Jesus is Lord and they will give their lives to relay that belief like Peter did thousands of years before now.

This belief caused the people to devote themselves to the apostles teaching and to fellowship. It caused them to sell their property and possessions and give to anyone who had need. It pushed them to meet in the temple courts and eat together every day with their fellow believers.

And this belief, when believed and surrendered to God, will cause the Holy Spirit to ignite the hearts of those in your home church and the supernatural can occur and God can do more through your home church than he has through any denomination, megachurch or movement that ever existed.

But first, remember this.

Jesus is Lord.

Chapter 1: You can't do it alone

I'm on vacation.   My first day of vacation, I heard yet another story of a pastor falling into a moral failure. In the last year, I've heard of or known at least six friends who have been let go from their church because of inappropriate actions regarding sex or money. The pressure of being a pastor in an institutional church is huge and the bigger the church gets, the more the pressure builds.

This is the life of someone whose job it is to make sure people come, give, and stay at the organization.

The person at the top is a person with influence and a person with influence is always looked at as a leader. The leader is someone who has it all together. They are focused, good, a visionary, and always knows what to do next. This leader is the kind of person that others want to be close to, and many times others make themselves close to that person simply because of their position.

Or over time, the person at the top begins to feel like they are not compensated the way they should be compensated so they find ways, even unethical, to compensate themselves despite the best financial practices the church has in place.

In a home church, it is no different, except one thing. In a home church (or even in a healthy institutional church), it is not up to the pastor or the staff to make the church grow, but it is the Holy Spirit's job to equip the people of God to bring in and call the unbeliever to become a part of His family.

If you want to start a home church, you believe that the church is not a one man or a one woman show, but many institutional churches lend themselves toward this way of thinking. They focus on the pastor's teaching or the youth pastor's leading or the number of sales tactics that are *necessary* for a growing church.

But a home church works and acts as a true body. Let me ask you this, Do the churches you've attended move this way:

"The human body has many parts, but the many parts make up one whole body. So it is with the body of Christ. Some of us are Jews, some are Gentiles, some are slaves, and some are free. But we have all been baptized into one body by one Spirit, and we all share the same Spirit. Yes, the body has many different parts, not just one part. If the foot says, "I am not a part of the body because I am not a hand," that does not make it any less a part of the body. And if the ear says, "I am not part of the body because I am not an eye," would that make it any less a part of the body? If the whole body were an eye, how would you hear? Or if your whole body were an ear, how would you smell anything?

How strange a body would be if it had only one part! Yes, there are many parts, but only one body. The eye can never say to the hand, "I don't need you." The head can't say to the feet, "I don't need you." In fact, some parts of the body that seem weakest and least important are

actually the most necessary. And the parts we regard as less honorable are those we clothe with the greatest care. So we carefully protect those parts that should not be seen, while the more honorable parts do not require this special care. So God has put the body together such that extra honor and care are given to those parts that have less dignity. This makes for harmony among the members, so that all the members care for each other. If one part suffers, all the parts suffer with it, and if one part is honored, all the parts are glad. All of you together are Christ's body, and each of you is a part of it."
1 Corinthians 12:12-17, 19-27 NLT

Now here's where this gets really tricky. You've probably heard institutional church pastors preach on this and talk about how important the door holders and the tech people are during the Sunday morning service, and as people they *are* super important. But the gifts that Paul talks about regarding the church are primarily spiritual.

Every church should be loaded with different people who God has gifted for spiritual practice in order to equip, grow, and disciple its members. The same is true not only with individual churches but also with the church as a whole.

So when you start your home church, please understand that **you can't do it alone.** You need people around you, mentors and peers, who can build you up and encourage you to become the home church you are called to be. If you try to do everything yourself, you are like the eye that says to the hand, "I don't need you!"

I don't care if you are an introvert or an extrovert, you need to find people to communicate one on one with both in person and by phone or face time. Here are some ideas for connecting with others:

*Face time or Skype every few days with someone.

*Meet weekly at a coffee shop with the same person.

*Have breakfast or dinner at least monthly with one or a group of people.

*Make a point to text your church every day.

*Use the Marco Polo app and video message a person you're close to or want to be close to every day.

*Ask someone or a few people in your home church to stay after everyone and build your relationship with them.

There is no shortage of things you can do to grow as a pastor through the relationships God has put in your life, but the most important principle to learn from this chapter is that under no circumstances can you start a home church alone. You need others to go ahead of you and along side of you to go on the journey. As the ghost athlete in "Field of Dreams" said in the corn husks of Iowa, "If you build it (those relationships), they will come."

Perhaps I took that out of context, but onward we go!

Questions for the journey

Are you an extrovert or an introvert?

Who are you pouring into now even before you have decided to start a home church?

Are pastors getting together in your area?

What one or two couples are starting your home church with you?

What pastor or church leader (home or institutional) has recommended you serve as a pastor?

Chapter 2: Discipline

One of the fruits of the Spirit, the last one listed in fact, is self control.   Another way to say that is self discipline.   Self discipline is the single most important human quality for starting a home church.   It's as important as starting an institutional church.   You cannot start a home church because you *think it's a good idea* or you're mad at the church you left. You must start a house church because the Spirit of God moves in you to make disciples and teach them the commands of Jesus. Then those disciples transform into leaders and do the same.

Unfortunately these transformations don't always happen miraculously.   Miracles do happen, but this specific transformation of discipleship only happens over the course of time as someone who actively follows Jesus intentionally pours in to someone else desiring to learn how to follow Jesus.

Like any successful transformation, this involves intentional and regular activity.   Jesus spent three years developing his disciples and turning them into imperfect spiritual *superheroes.* In the course of his earthly lifetime though, he never saw their success.

So how do you intentionally start a home church using self discipline? The same way you start any church, organization, or venture.   Here are three tools to nurture self discipline as you get started.

Proper Planning

Many times people starting home churches have had less success in the area of organization than those in the institutional church.   Unfortunately, planning isn't less important because something is smaller.   In fact, in order to maintain growth and order, planning when starting and continuing your home church is probably more important than in an institutional setting.

Before you meet for the first time, sit down and plan out your goals, objectives, and specific details like how often, when, and where you will meet (officially).

Sometimes when we think about home church settings we think organically to a point where we make decisions based on what works best for those who may be attending.   Remember you are the discipler and the teacher.   You are the pastor.   Of course that doesn't mean you are a dictator, but people gravitate toward order and security.

Years ago in an institutional church I pastored, I changed a Wednesday night service to a Wednesday night family night. One Sunday morning I told a mother about the changes and invited her and her family to attend.   She seemed interested and even excited about the new format and asked what time it would be.   When I told her she frowned and told me she worked and it would need to be later for her family to be able to attend.

In my youth, I assured her I could change the time and actually did change it.   Shockingly, that lady and her family never attended the family night.   The time objection was an excuse and she assumed I would never change it simply for her family. We were such a small church, changing the time was an easy thing to do. I learned a valuable lesson as a young pastor. People prioritize what they want to prioritize. I realize not everyone can attend every time a church meets, but if someone wants to become a disciple, they will make adjustments to be discipled. Also, as we will learn later, the house church doesn't do *once-a-week* anyways, so there should be plenty of opportunities for everyone to learn, grow, and follow Jesus.

Regular Rallies

The only reason I wrote it that way is because everyone knows good pastors alliterate their points. Institutional churches meet every Sunday morning (or Saturday morning in some denominations). Some evangelical megachurches proudly say, "It's all about the weekend." The truth is that the church being focused on one day hurts the identity of a disciple carrying out her mission seven days a week, but meeting once a week at least should be mandatory for any home church.

Last summer though, as we started thinking about home churches, meeting once a week proved to be difficult when we weren't intentional about planning a regular time. However, if I were starting a home church today, I would plan for a minimum of meeting two days. To be honest, *Once-a-week* Christianity hasn't produced disciples who will love and die for Jesus or His church. As I mentioned before, Acts 2 speaks of followers of Jesus meeting in the temple, meeting daily in one another's homes, and having all things in common. This type of communal living, or at least something similar to the great American family, is necessary for the love it takes to be a disciple.

We get dressed up, go to a church, worship for an hour or so, then head home and live the rest of our week out filling our schedules with work, Netflix, kids sports, and landscaping. When we take a step to serving at church for an extra hour or so of what might amount to holding a door or playing an instrument, we call that discipleship. Or when we attend a small group, we talk ourselves into believing we are really "doing life together" and "killing it for Jesus".

Communication Culture

In an institutional church, people go to church, then they go home, and sometimes they communicate with someone from their church and sometimes they don't but the next week they go back again for church.

A good pastor or small group leader communicates regularly with people in their church or group. But if they don't it's no big deal, especially in an area where everyone goes to church. In a home church environment, however, constant communication between all members is vital to continued growth. Each disciple is important to the overall health of the body and the body cannot function properly without the input of each disciple.

In a home church, there are no spectators or cheerleaders, but only people committed to advancing the kingdom of God in their church, community, and in the world. This philosophy means Lone Ranger Christians are not a thing the way they can be in the institutional church.

In America, we've taken individualism and privacy to new extremes, calling these things 'rights'. This is not the way of the disciple. It's possible you have built up habits in your life that have inadvertently pushed you away from the way Jesus calls us to, and towards your rights as American citizens. If so, build up disciplines that help you communicate more clearly, meet regularly, and plan properly.

If you don't, your house church will not last very long.

Questions for the journey

1. Would others say you are a person who has self control or self discipline?

2.   What tools do you use to ensure that you remain organized in your life and in your home?

3. Do you see yourself scheduling one time a week with your church or several times a week?

4. How many times a week do you reach out to those in your inner circle right now?

Chapter 3: Hospitality

As a pastor, my wife and I regularly hosted a small group. Each week we prepared not just the schedule for the meeting, but also our home. Typically we spent hours cleaning the nooks and crannies, vacuuming and mopping the floors, setting up the background music, lighting a scented candle, and ensuring that those attending the group felt comfortable.

Of course none of that is necessary for an effective event, but what is necessary is the gift of hospitality being exercised within the body. Peter says in his first letter to believers in Eastern Europe that they should 'continue to show deep love for each other' and to 'cheerfully share your home with those who need a meal or a place to stay.'

The important thing about hospitality is embedded in what Peter's last sentence: "Share your home."

Hospitality is acting as if your home is not yours only, but also is the home of anyone who is in it.

In our day of consumerism, materialism, and individualism, hospitality has become less important to people, so we tend to stay away from other people's stuff and worse, we tend to keep people away from our stuff. But our stuff is not ours in the first place. It is God's. As stewards of his possessions, believers are called to share the things we have for His glory and for ministry purposes. Friends of mine, Garret and Susan Walker are experts in the area of hospitality. For years I have watched and experienced them show hospitality in ways that show it as a gifting and not just something they do. The rest of this section is Garret's philosophy on hospitality, and I hope it encourages you as you prepare to start your home church.

HOSPITALITY: The Art and Science of Opening Your Home

We've all had occasion to drop-in on people at their homes. From parties and holidays to casual drinks or borrowing sugar, there are boundless opportunities to experience the hospitality of others. The variety and types of visits typically elicit a degree of anxious response in both host and guest. Returning a baking dish is far less daunting for most than arriving at a dinner party with a dish full of main course or far worse; salad, when you're 30 minutes late. And, having someone pop in to tell you your car's interior light is on has far less expectation on your disposition than hosting the Super Bowl.

Suffice to say we tend to be a bit more comfortable accepting invitations than doling them out. There's far more to be concerned about when providing friendly, warm, and generous treatment than receiving it. If you take a minute to imagine your home being the focus of a gathering, it isn't difficult to make a list of 10 or more things that require some attention or preparation. The first of our senses to satisfy is the eye. It's completely normal to instinctually and reflexively be concerned about the appearance of your home. If you're being totally honest, half the items on your "to do" list are related to the condition of your home. Some of you will even dismiss the possibility of hosting guests – never mind strangers – because you're self-conscious of the type and size of your home, dingy furniture, an old ugly carpet, or the lack of parking. All of these things have the potential to put off a guest…no matter what!

The truth about quality hospitality though is that it isn't physical or material at all. Being a good host is always about attitude. Your spirit about hosting is what gives life to the meaning of hospitality, "a warm, friendly, and generous reception and treatment of guests or strangers." There's no way to escape or fake this reality. Surprisingly, being anxious or nervous is not the greatest put-off nor the biggest obstacle to expressing hospitality. Being hyper-focused on what your guests think of your possessions is. And by that, I mean being obsessed with insisting your guests judge you by the quality and quantity of your things. That attitude will always come shining through and folks aren't really upset that you have more or nicer things than them, they resent that you're expecting them to think it's important. What's worse than being proudly puffed up by your material status is being ashamed of what you have. Never apologize for the means by which you live.

This is truly at the core of our fretting over having people *over*. We lose touch with our essence and the place we occupy in God's kingdom. It must grieve the Spirit to lose control of self and embrace our petty fears at the expense of the many fruits we have to offer. Now, there's also the truth that some folks just aren't gifted with natural hospitable instincts. It does take some work; not just with attitude, but with the pragmatic preparation and common cultural attention to detail.

Communicate well

Advance notice should be part of an invitation. This is, of course, highly subjective with the goal being to ensure guests have enough time to schedule a "yes". Try not to wait less than a week before your gathering. There are some spontaneous opportunities to host and you should be self-aware enough to manage your response. This is where you might want to check your anxiety about your home not being *tidy*.

...Next to godliness

You never want a guest to ask "where are your cats?"when they can't be seen. Smells are powerful things. Your home doesn't need to smell great, just not rank. In fact, it's best that you don't go overboard with strong scents as some folks are sensitive to such. Your beloved Peppermint-Pine-Gardenia candle may set a stellar mood in the loo, but not so savory when blended with your meticulously prepared, aromatic porchetta. In general, if you desire to become better at
hospitality, one great practical cornerstone is a clean house

Delegate

Guests typically love to contribute. If you're having more than one couple or person over and people expect to eat, do take on the bulk of that responsibility
and suggest there are some holes to fill. Most people will ask what they can contribute, but if you're not comfortable making suggestions or delegating, don't. Food makes a gathering more special, but it shouldn't be the focus of hospitality. Some people just aren't foodies and they shouldn't be pressured...including you.

Fake it till you make it

Greeting is the key to disarming your guests' anxiety (and yours). Your mood and expressions and attitude are infectious. A certain amount of faking is good
if you must, but be prepared to be honest about that. I don't always feel up to it on the days we host our regular group and sharing a bit about what has me
down is an authentic connection. Caution though; don't play martyr. Your guests will want to leave.

Set Parameters

Be sure everyone knows when the party is over. Do not be shy about setting an end time and sticking with it. Like my favorite tavern does; set the clocks ahead. Leave some transition time so this doesn't get uncomfortable. If you want everyone out by 10, tell them the gathering ends at 9:30.

 Lastly, take this bold and necessary step as you consider hosting a gathering at your home. Stand in the middle of each room and pray thanksgiving to God out loud. Tell him about your fears and needs and desire to use *His* home. Ask his blessing on each space. Growing in hospitality is an extension of all the Spiritual Fruits; and *thankfulness* is a great place to start.

Questions for the journey

1. Does hospitality come naturally to you and your family?

2. When you start a home church, is it important to you to host it at your home or will it be somewhere else?

3. Do you have any strange smells in your home that could be distracting for people who join you?

4. Is your attitude when people visit your home distracted about the circumstances or welcoming?

5. How are you in communicating boundaries to others?

Chapter 4: Family

In ancient times, families moved across the earth nomadically, making homes for themselves where they could live out their days and feel safe and comfortable. Over time, those families became tribes, those tribes became villages, those villages became nations, and those nations became empires.

Of course today we have each of these, but we still value the cornerstone of these groups - the family - more than any other unit available to us.

This was never more true than in Ancient Israel. The very foundation of the nation was rooted in family - Abraham, Isaac, and Jacob's family, that is. Jacob's twelve sons expanded and formed the basis for the way the tribes separated and united when their large family morphed into a world empire. But through all of that growth, the family of Israel highlighted the way the people thought about others in general. There was family and then there was everyone else.

Jesus, of course, was born into this Jewish world, but as he taught, he did so with a new vision: That family is thicker than blood. He understood that people had an *us four and no more* mindset, and he challenged people to love and care for those outside of their family unit. To clarify, Jesus wasn't saying the family is not important. He was saying, "Family is more than just who your bloodline happens to be."

Today we have a tendency to be no different than any culture who focuses on family and at the same time ignores those who don't think, act, or live like our family. Yet we are called by God to reach out and treat people outside of our bloodline like they are family.

The Family of God

In John 17, Jesus prays a prayer to his Father focusing on his disciples. In verse 21, he says, "I pray that they will all be one-as you are in me Father, and I am in you. And may they be in us so that the world will believe you sent me." I don't know about you, but when I think about the church, all of the church *being one* is a fantastic pipe dream, but not grounded in reality. There are 33,000 denominations in the world, many of them small and segregated from the others.

At the same time, more and more people are leaving the institutional church because of mismanagement, lack of discipleship, and a hunger for power (lack of humility) displayed by church leaderships across the board.

Jesus told his disciples that one of the ways people will know that you are a disciple of his is your love for one another. Can you imagine what he would think today about the boundaries and walls put up by the different *sides* of his followers? People doing more fighting than serving one another and putting their beliefs ahead of their behavior toward their fellow Christ followers.

If you want to start a home church, it is imperative that the group you bring together, evangelize, and disciple, love each other as well as any family member you've ever had. I don't mean a little love. I mean loving in a way that people literally know that you are a follower of Christ by the love expressed between those of you who are following Jesus together. I mean the kind of bone-jarring love that causes people to join churches instead of complain about them.   And I mean sacrificing for your brothers and sisters and that sacrifice then causes others to desire to be a part of that family.

Let me be clear, I don't think you should love your fellow believers because others will see you and want to be a part of the family of God. I believe the Spirit of God allows you to love others supernaturally as you access his power, and the fruit of that love then is the catalyst by which that same spirit calls others into God's family.

I have spent the better part of my life serving in and being a part of church communities, and this one thing is always true - When I pour myself into God's family, I create and become a part of a family as close or closer than my own birth family. This is significant because many times we treat the church like a social gathering or a weekly activity, when in reality, the church should be another name for family.

I have a friend who leads a home church. Each week on Tuesday night my friend prepares a lesson, communicates with everyone, then they all gather together with their families and have church.

The problem?   Everyone still has their own institutional church. Many times they will not attend their Tuesday night "service" because their institutional church has a Tuesday or a Wednesday event.

My friend came to me discouraged and wondering what he should do. I told him to "communicate to his church that this was church and not something to be cancelled because of another church event. We either are family or we are not. It's not that we can't have some nights that we cancel, it's that we have come to a place where our church is considered a night or a morning that is the problem."

Church isn't a service or a building or a worship time or a day or a night. Church is a people - God's people - who gather faithfully with one another and encourage one another towards love and good deeds.

I want to warn you right now, especially if you have a background in the institutional church. In order for your home church to feel like a family, you must push away the tendency to use people to accomplish your tasks. For years now, the church has morphed into a production based event, which means many volunteer hours are needed to make the event happen. Overwhelmingly, those volunteers end up coming from the church body, and are taught to use their gifts by holding a door open, playing a guitar, or babysitting a child. Please don't mishear me. Those actions can be using their gifts, but those things become systematized and the gifts end up becoming more important than the disciple exercising the gifts.

If you want to start a home church, begin exercising your mind to treat fellow believers like they are your family. Become intimately aware of their needs. Serve them when they need love and when they don't. Find yourself close to them when they are burdened by difficulty. And find ways to communicate with them about their lives a part from the structure of a program and all throughout the week, several times a day if necessary (or not).

1. Have you looked at your church family in the past as family?

2. What are some ways that you can exercise church unity outside of your home church?

3. What is one practice you can use to ensure that your home church doesn't become a once a week gathering?

4. How does your family act around your church family?

Chapter 5: The Bible

Everything I know about God comes from the Bible. That is not true of Abraham. This tells me two things. As a believer, I need to take the Bible seriously. It also tells me that the Bible is not the only way we get to know God.

So let's take that paragraph and break it down.

Everything I know about God comes from the Bible.

This is almost true. Of course, Scripture tells us we can see God in nature, but the way we worship and the things we believe about Him generally emanates from the source known as the Holy Bible. It is within the sixty six books and two testaments that the writers explain who God is through their experience, and more importantly, through God's own spirit.

So there is a certain authority that comes from scripture. The question then becomes what kind of authority? Is it the type we take literally and each command that God gives in it is a command for us today? Is it a rule book that we look to build boundaries around our lives so we maintain a firm grasp of what not do in life?

N.T Wright asks a similar questions in a sermon he gave called, *How can the Bible be authoritative?* He says:

"When people in the church talk about authority they are very often talking about controlling people or situations. They want to make sure that everything is regulated properly, that the church does not go off the rails doctrinally or ethically, that correct ideas and practices are upheld and transmitted to the next generation. 'Authority' is the place where we go to find out the correct answers to key questions such as these. This notion, however, runs into all kinds of problems when we apply it to the Bible. Is that really what the Bible is for? Is it there to control the church? Is it there simply to look up the correct answers to questions that we, for some reason, already know?"

The answer is obvious. The Bible does not exist to control the church. So then why does it exist and is it indeed authoritative?

The easy answer is that the Bible is authoritative because God Himself is authoritative. God said... God created...God breathed.... The good news is that God still does those things. He still speaks and creates and breathes, and it is our job as His faithful subjects to get to know Him in a way that properly interprets how He communicates with us.

This requires us to get to know God by getting to know the Bible. More on this later.

That is not true of Abraham

This probably does not come as a shock to you, but Abraham had no Bible. He had no law or scroll pointing him to how to behave or how to think about God. But scripture tells us the story of this Biblical stallion.

Abraham, or Abram (his given name), somehow developed the type of relationship with God where God communicated to him, and he obeyed. He didn't always understand, nor did he have anything written down that fortified his trust in a God he could not see, however, God communicated to Abram, and Abram listened and obeyed.

God told him to leave his extended family and go somewhere else. Abram took his wife and a few others and left. God gave him land and made him successful. Abram and his wife grew old. God promised him a son. Genesis 15:6 says, "Abram believed the Lord, and the Lord counted him as righteous because of his faith."

In other words, Abram's connection with God had nothing to do with Scripture, but with his own personal faith. It was that faith that made him right with God. So it wasn't his behavior that pleased God, or even a moral code he adhered to, but his ability to understand God's place in his life, despite not being able to see Him. He was not perfect, like so many of the other Biblical heroes, but his faith propelled him to be an example to us of how to get to know and follow after God.

As a believer, I need to take the Bible seriously

Just because Abram didn't need to have a Bible to know God doesn't mean we can ignore it. The Bible is authoritative and must be poured over by those of us who consider ourselves disciples of Jesus.

Far too many followers have very little faith, and that lack of faith leads to a lack of desire to read and comprehend his Word.

The Bible is looked at like a rule book, or worse, a book of little encouragements to get us through the day, instead of God's authoritative word.

When you start a home church, you should decide to take the Bible seriously in a way that most do not have the guts to do. It is not something to be worshipped or something to be taken extremely literal. The Bible is not even simply something to be read. Instead, it is a book, that when you read it, will begin to read you.

With every Spirit-driven reading of the Bible, God's own Spirit will begin to communicate with you. And not only you, but as you teach those in your home church, the same should happen with each member of the body. Your faith in God and relationship with God causes you to read His Word, and then His Spirit brings something to light you would have never seen without his power. "For, 'Who can know the Lord's thoughts? Who knows enough to teach him?' But we understand these things, for we have the mind of Christ." 1 Corinthians 2:16 says.

The Bible is not the only way to get to know God

We close our chapter with this thought. Though the Bible needs to be taken seriously by everyone in your home church, and it should have a prominent place within the gatherings, it should be known that the Bible is not the only way to get to know God.

For your church to access the power of God, it must connect with God's Spirit before any reading of His Word. When the Bible becomes a text book, it is like any other book anyone can read, order, or check out at a library. The Bible is not a deity, and it is a collection of words and phrases. Coupled with the Holy Spirit, though, life change can and will happen.

Faith, prayer, using spiritual gifts, holiness, and taking risks should all be connected with the Bible as tools to get to know the God you are worshiping together. Psalms 119:105 says, "Your word is a lamp to guide my feet and a light for my path." Think of it this way. If you are outside at night trying to get somewhere, a light is really important and should be taken seriously. But ultimately you can find where you're going without the light.

As a home church, make the Bible an integral part of your lives, but stop short of worshiping it and becoming legalistic due to one or two people's dogmatic interpretations of it. When that happens, dysfunction reigns, and reigning is most certainly the role of Jesus in the church.

Questions for the journey

1. When did you begin to read the Bible and how did those who taught ti to you read it?

2. What are ways that you build your faith in God apart from Scripture?

3. How will you fend off the influence of those in your group who don't take the Bible seriously?

4.   How much do you read the Bible a week?   This is important because unless you have a firm understanding of the Bible, it will be difficult to start a home church.

Chapter 6: Mission

"You are the light of the world—like a city on a hilltop that cannot be hidden." - Matthew 5:14 NLT

If you're still reading this, I assume you're not one of those people who stands up in a pulpit and screams about the evils of rock music or that the Bible version you preach from is the only one sanctioned by God himself. Don't laugh, I know a few of those people.

And though there are people who act like this or who stand outside of the funerals of US soldiers holding up signs that say any number of outrageous things, we are called to be a city on a hilltop that 'cannot be hidden.'. How we are to be that kind of a person, however, is anyones guess. The only thing we can do is follow the Spirit's leading, read scripture, and analyze the lives of those who went before us. In his own words, Paul spoke humbly and 'without lofty words or impressive wisdom." He built imperfect communities. But in the meantime, they were loved to an extent that being kicked out of one of them was considered punishment. This could only be true if there was such great love and service happening, that everyone in the communities knew the impact they were making on the world.

Their mission was serving, and in fact, serving a community that turned around and punished them for being who they were and for believing what they believed. Many of them were beaten, imprisoned, stoned, shunned, and killed for their beliefs, no matter how much they loved on those who hated them.

So when you start your home church, what will your mission be? How will you serve your community? Will you be intentional about taking care of the needs of your neighbors, friends, and family?

Not only must your church maintain its fluidity by taking care of the needs of those closest to you , you must also take care of the specific needs of your greater community as well. Of course, the needs in that area are going to be much greater than anything you or your home church can squelch, but with the right focus, a good sized dent can be made in the problem.

Many churches, choosing to focus their efforts only on telling people about Jesus, outsource their missional steps to non profit organizations. At first glance this is not a huge issue because many of these organizations are church driven, being led by those in the body of Christ. But churches, desiring to maintain their own institutional power and standing, will keep people who should be out leading the way in serving and social justice, and put them in influential yet stagnant positions within their church structure.

The home church, however, positions each disciple to serve within the context of outward mission and not inward system. For instance, suppose the mission of your home church is to adopt a local and underfunded public elementary school in your area, and your church does that with all your might. Then one family in your church decides God is calling them to move on and serve in a different capacity.

The institutional church might balk at such a move, especially if it affects the systematic way things currently run. The home church pushes those families in a way that lovingly challenges them to go and serve and follow after God's leading. This encourages growth in every believer, and discourages the focus of the church from staying on the institution, or worse, a figurehead leader within the institution.

So how do you find your mission as a home church?

You pray

Not just you, but your entire church gathers together, prays and asks God to lead and Guide them to a mission that, when they act it out, accomplishes God's greater purposes in the world.

Please don't try to make a mission happen without first asking God. This is preposterous in general for a Christian, but as a pastor, it is ecclesiastical suicide. Your home church needs God as much as any other church needs Him. You need His leading and His guiding, and you certainly need his instruction.

You study

Have you ever studied the area you live to see what is the greatest need in your community? If not, get on that! Homelessness, addiction, materialism, pornography, bitterness? The problems around you could be any number of things, but you probably have a tool in your house that with a few clicks of a button, you can know what those problems are.

It's possible you already are being led in that direction as you have prayed, but make sure to research the biggest needs in your area and allow God's Spirit to work in that research and move in your group.

Make sure others in the group are doing their research too. The more minds studying, the better to see how God can work through your home church.

You discuss

You don't talk your way out of what God is leading you to do, but you discuss what and how God is leading you to act. Anyone can say God is leading you into this or that, but only a truly confident disciple can look a doubter in the eyes, and without getting defensive, discuss opposition, doubt, or someone else's God ordained plans.

I went to a Christian college in Florida, and during my time there, hundreds of people I knew were certain that God led them to break up with their boyfriend or girlfriend. In reality, most of those people realized the person they spent most of their time with currently was not the kind of person they wanted to be with for the rest of their lives, and that was okay, but the suggestion that God did not want the relationship to exist somehow made the breakup easier to digest for those involved.

Discussion, and in particular, healthy discussion, allows for all the cards to be placed on the table, and in disagreement, the church can always go back to praying to ensure God is the primary source of decision making when it comes to the mission. When you make a decision, you can also discuss the how-tos of where to go next in defeating the giants you now see before you and your community.

It's time to act

When I say act, I don't mean do a service project that will make a small dent in the mission you are undertaking, but I mean act in a way that your whole lives are now given over to accomplishing this God given mission. The greatest world changers devoted themselves to a single focused mission and worked to solve those problems over the course of their whole lives.

Many groups decide to do a monthly or a quarterly service project here or there, but that's not what I'm talking about here. By mission, I'm referring to something God has given your home church, that if your home church doesn't act on, the world will be or will continue to be, a darker world.

It's time to act, world changers. As you start your home church, remember to grab ahold of the mission God has for your small part of the body of Christ.

Questions for the journey

1. Have you ever poured yourself into a community problem and made a huge dent in the project?

2. Without thinking about it, what one societal problem do you feel impassioned to fix?

3.   What are the top three problems in your current community?

Chapter 7: Generosity and how it works

One of the huge advantages of the home church is the focus disciples can have in regards to their finances, but it can also be the most confusing for someone starting out. A popular chart for institutional church consultants goes like this:

Staffing - 40%

Grounds and facilities - 30%

Ministry - 20%

Tithe - 10%

That breakdown is the general percentage that the income an institutional church brings in should land regarding the church's finances. So in an American church, at least 70% of the church income goes to keep the institution alive, and the other 30% (maybe) goes to seeing ministry happen. The reason I say maybe is because in one church I had occasion to visit on Easter Sunday, the projectors used draped not only the screens set up on the back of the stage, but brilliantly shone around the entire front half of the walls as well. The cost of the updated projectors was around $40,000 to the church, and could very easily have been put into the "ministry" category.

I'm not judging the idea of paying pastors or keeping buildings looking nice, but the reality is that the church talks a lot about seeing hungry people get fed and clothing the naked and generally taking care of people, but very few churches are using their finances to make any kind of a dent in the hurt and pain around them.

In the home church, however, 100% of the incoming funds can be given to help the poor and the hurting, the weak and the downtrodden.   No one is getting paid.   The church has no building to meet in. And there is no need to buy a projector or Bose speakers. If no one in the group has an acoustic guitar or can play the keyboard, then everyone can just sing, and the joy in their voices will do just fine.

So how do the finances work in a home church?

Accountability is everything

Just because the house church might be small and we may not be talking about thousands of dollars a week, that doesn't mean we shouldn't take the appropriate steps to being fiscally responsible with the church's money. Here are some important internal controls to insure that accountability is happening with the finances of your church.

*Make sure that at least two people are in custody of the offering at all times until it is safely deposited into the bank.

*Promptly deposit all money into the bank when it is received.

*Assign someone other than those who handle the offering to reconcile the bank statements on a monthly basis.

Get a Bank Account

I'm not legalistic when it comes to this point, and I can see how things would be easier in certain areas when it comes to giving some cash and not thinking about it any more, but in only a few short steps, your home church can have a dba (doing business as), which is necessary for a bank account. In many states, it's as easy as going to your town or city clerk's website, downloading an dba form, filling it out, and turning it in, along with most likely paying a filing fee. Soon you'll hear back from the office and be able to go to the bank and get an account for your home church. You'll have to choose a name of course, but that's the fun part!

Here are the steps (in many states) to create a dba so you can get a bank account:

*Download a DBA "Doing business as" form from your town web site.

*Fill out the form, and get it notarized.

*Turn the form in to your town or city. Their may be a filing fee.

*Take the form to the bank and open an account.

*I would suggest getting a business checking and savings with no fees.

You should have a treasurer

You have people with different gifts in your house church. Inevitably one of them will have some sort of financial background or be good with details and organization. Make that person your treasurer. As a pastor of a home church, there is no need for you to be in charge of the money. You are a pastor, not a dictator. You want to stay above reproach when it comes to money and your church, so please consider handing the reigns of the bank account to someone else. Even if you don't have a bank account, you can appoint someone to oversee the financial aspects of your home church. This may not be the best argument, but even Jesus had a treasurer. Jesus certainly knew Judas Iscariot was going to betray him, but still gave him that position.

Pray as a group how God wants your money to be given out

There are people in need. There are people all over the place who need resources and your church, combined together, has some of the resources to help them. It may not be a lot, but you have collected money to be given out so those in need can be loved on and helped through a hard time in their life. But there are those who also only want a hand out. There are those who are dishonest with their money, and you don't want to risk not being able to give money to someone in need because someone in greed tells you a sob story. Read the following story in Acts 5:1-11:

"But there was a certain man named Ananias who, with his wife, Sapphira, sold some property. He brought part of the money to the apostles, claiming it was the full amount. With his wife's consent, he kept the rest. Then Peter said, "Ananias, why have you let Satan fill your heart? You lied to the Holy Spirit, and you kept some of the money for yourself. The property was yours to sell or not sell, as you wished. And after selling it, the money was also yours to give away. How could you do a thing like this? You weren't lying to us but to God!" As soon as Ananias heard these words, he fell to the floor and died. Everyone who heard about it was terrified. Then some young men got up, wrapped him in a sheet, and took him out and buried him. About three hours later his wife came in, not knowing what had happened. Peter asked her, "Was this the price you and your husband received for your land?" "Yes," she replied, "that was the price." And Peter said, "How could the two of you even think of conspiring to test the Spirit of the Lord like this? The young men who buried your husband are just outside the door, and they will carry you out, too." Instantly, she fell to the floor and died. When the young men came in and saw that she was dead, they carried her out and buried her beside her husband. Great fear gripped the entire church and everyone else who heard what had happened."

Jesus and his disciples took money very seriously, and so should you and your home church. Peter was sensitive to those lying about their finances. I'm not suggesting you have the Holy Spirit kill those who try to take advantage of your church, but I do believe you should go to him with every financial situation and ask him what his will in in regards to that decision your church needs to make.

And along the way, please be careful. Money can be a temptation that even the most honest people can fall into, so be mindful of your own pitfalls with money and if possible, distance yourself from it.

Questions for the journey

1. Have you seen people take advantage of money in your past church experiences?

2. Think about an amazing story where you've seen the church really come through for people in need.

3. How important is it to you that people in your home church give or tithe?

4. Do you think the church handling money is a good idea or a bad temptation waiting to happen?

Chapter 8: Evangelism

Evangelism is not simple. Entire books can be written about the topic and what it is and how to do it. But this is just one chapter, and I'm assuming if you've read this far in this book, you already know what it is. The question we'll touch on in this chapter is how to help your new home church share the good news of Jesus with those around them.

In the last 40 plus years that I've been around, evangelism tactics have taken many shapes and varieties including door-to-door visitation, Christian apologetics, or the more recent approach, "point person". Point person is the method of evangelism that encourages believers to invite their friends and family to church, and when they do so, their friends and family will hear the gospel in a clear way by a professional point person who is gifted at sharing the good news of Jesus.

Theoretically this is an excellent method, however, many drawbacks surround this theory. The main problem is the bottleneck it creates when Christians abdicate their role as believers to "go and make disciples of all nations...."

In reality, the home church sets itself up for being the right kind of church in regards to evangelism just by being a home church. Because the home church is small, it negates the idea of those who come to church as spectators instead of being the church and stepping into the role of full on participants.

Evangelism is best accomplished when the members of the church are trained and devoted to sharing their faith with their community. So the home church pastor not only challenges their members to share their faith, but teaches them to do so and allows them opportunity to practice sharing their story with one another.

One great curriculum I used for my home church held a time during each meeting when the members would share their faith story with one another, and after they did it, they did it again. They did it again not so it would be robotic but so that when they shared it, it would sound comfortable coming out of their mouths.

No matter how you decide to share your faith story though, here are the elements that need to be in your story:

Pray and ask God to prepare you and those around you

As usual, prayer is a vital and often overlooked part of evangelism. There is no drier ground in reaching people than a field harvested without the rain of spiritual tears being shed for those who are lost. Crying out to God for those you care about is not a weakness, but his strength is made perfect in our weakness. How long have you asked God to reach your friends or family? How long have you asked Him to create fertile ground around you? And yet we want God to use us and to see people come to Him. Do we think we can make that happen with our stunning answers and amazing worship services? Take some time regularly as a home church and pray that God would stir in the hearts of those around us a need for Him.

Start your faith story with your church

Your story is powerful. Anytime God works in a life and brings someone from darkness to light it is powerful. So why do we run from sharing what God has done for us? Start with the moment you realized you needed Jesus, and share the circumstances around that moment. How old were you when you came to faith? What did you have? What kinds of things did you put your trust in before you gave it to God? If you came to Christ as a child, did you walk away from him after the fact? All of these questions and others are important questions you should answer when you share your story with those around you.   Your story is the porch light connecting an unbeliever to a new home with Jesus.

Share why everyone needs Christ

Living in extreme wealth in heaven is not a good reason to come to Christ, nor is the idea that your life will be blissful if you give the keys of your life to him. So why should those you're sharing your faith with come to Jesus and be a part of his body? You'll have to explain the good news very clearly before you finish. Paul gave it succinctly in 1 Corinthians 15 when he said, "I passed on to you what was most important and what had also been passed on to me. Christ died for our sins, just as the Scriptures said. He was buried, and he was raised from the dead on the third day, just as the Scriptures said. He was seen by Peter and then by the Twelve. After that, he was seen by more than 500 of his followers at one time, most of whom are still alive, though some have died." Share why that is good news.

Surrender doesn't grow on trees, but it does produce fruit

Finally, call the person to repent and surrender their lives to Christ. This is not altogether easy for someone to do in our society because we have been programmed to let people be who they are, but in any other area of our lives, we don't do that. In our physical bodies, we realize the importance of exercise and occasionally call others to join us in that endeavor. In the areas of philosophy or education, we challenge one another to better ourselves by researching what we do not know. If someone is sick, we share information that could make them better with the proper treatment. So if we know following Jesus is the right way, what do we have to be timid or apologetic about? Call the person you're talking to to repentance and to surrender their lives to become a disciple of Jesus.

Throughout this process, we must move away from worrying about hurting others feelings, and be bold as we communicate the love, grace, and forgiveness of God to a world that does not want us, but who does need us. Your home church is not just a group who meets together once a week, but a walking group of disciples bent on turning the world back to its creator.

1. Have you ever led someone to Jesus?

2. What does someone spiritually gifted in evangelism look like? Think about someone you know, and ask God to bring someone like that to your church.

3. How will you keep evangelism in the forefront of your church's mind?

Chapter 9: Other Brothers and Sisters

Most Christians today have a church, which makes the possibility of a believer coming to your home church, and that being their "only church", not very good. Our pride tells us that we want our church to be the only church around, but in the process of starting and leading a home church, we must remember that every one who confesses Jesus Christ as Lord is part of our church.   It is only because of our culture that churches become organizations that eventually become institutions that eventually become memorials.

The church that Jesus instituted, however, is a living organism that moves with the guidance of His Spirit to share the good news of Jesus wherever He leads us. It is not a social club or even a pillar of truth, but a movement that multiplies and extends its reach wherever it goes.

The home church must do better than the institutional church has done in regards to the way it treats its brothers and sisters outside of its little group. Believers who are believers that don't attend the home church are the same body as believers who attend your home church. They are no different.

I worked at a church once that had a group of core values, and one of those values were to "complete, and not compete" with the larger body of Christ. That sign was on the walls and frequently mentioned in messages from the stage. The longer I served in that church, however, the more I heard the leadership talk about how we as a church were going to dominate the world and how different our church was than others around us.

One time a fellow pastor from the area visited and sat through one of our services. A few weeks later, I asked my brother in the ministry what he thought of our church, and the first thing he mentioned to me was his disappointment that the speaking pastor spoke ill of a particular denomination during his sermon. I hadn't thought about that as I listened to the same speech because it had become common place for the pastor to use those types of illustrations.

An organization almost always leans toward differentiating itself from other organizations, but the home church has the ability to not do that, because it is not in the business of existing, and in fact, it is not in business at all. It exists solely to do what Christ asked us to do - nothing more and nothing less.

Earlier in this book, I mentioned my friend whose home church members all went to other churches on the weekends. The man or woman who starts a home church must put away the desire to manipulate others to do what they want them to do (which in this case might be to only attend the home church) and allow people freedom to live out their faith in multiple environments. After all, the body of Christ is vast and extends into several types of gathering places. So how do house churches connect with the greater body of Christ?

City Life

When Paul wrote his letters, he wrote them to churches in particular cities. Those churches served their cities and not their organizations. In other words, there were no First Baptists in Corinth, but only the church in Corinth. Presumably this was because the church was small at this point in time, but imagine if every church in a particular city looked at themselves not as First Baptist or Journey Church or North Point but instead, thought of themselves as Boston's church or Youngstown's church or a church in Dallas. But how would we differentiate ourselves from one another? I'm sure we'd figure it out. The fastest growing churches in the world right now are decentralized home churches going through persecution. They're not marketing and they have no web sites, but I'm sure they look at themselves as part of the family of God and view other groups similarly. Institutional churches could do a better job at this too, but that is for another book.

Leader Connect

The difference between a leader and someone who is not a leader shouldn't be such a huge gap in the kingdom of God. You can almost always tell a pastor or a leader in a church from someone who attends. But in reality, disciples are disciples and should act accordingly. One difference, however, at least initially as the home church gets started, is that the leader must train herself to connect with other leaders in other home churches and institutional churches. There must be a physical or communicative connection between churches in the larger body of Christ. So as you get started, make a point to find other home churches and pastors gatherings in the area and do your best to either attend the meetings or connect with pastors who do.   Then ask questions regarding the people, resources, and needs of the other churches. The body of Christ is one, and we need to begin acting like it.

Master-Teacher

In the business world, a boss or a group of bosses look around at his or her pool of underlings when its time for a promotion and pick the person who has displayed, from the vantage point of the boss, the highest qualities toward leadership. If you're wondering, this is not what Jesus did when he chose his disciples.   This is why the church is miserable at training up leaders. Jesus picked twelve men, and as far as we know, none of them were overly gifted to what they were called to accomplish. But they followed him. He was their leader and they followed him around for three years, failing and learning and failing some more and growing. There was never a choice when it came to whether or not they would lead. They had a calling and they were expected to follow their master/teacher and accomplish what he set out to accomplish. In your home church, you are not going to be speaking from a pulpit, but leading in a circle.   Everyone in your home church will be following you as you follow Jesus, and they should be expected to lead as they learn, fail, and grow. Eventually they should be able to go out and start their own groups, regardless of their personalities or what they've done in the past.

This is important because the church needs strong leadership, but it does not need hierarchies to accomplish its goals. Our flesh desires titles and positions and to be in charge, but the kingdom of God flourishes no matter who is in charge and no matter what church currently exists. As you start your home church, please understand you are a part of something much bigger than your church. You are a part of a great cloud of witnesses that has gone before you, and a huge group of people who will come after you. Starting with Jesus our Lord, we are all a part of his body. What a blessing! What a responsibility!

Questions for the journey

1.   Would you be more interested in meeting with other home church pastors or anyone who calls themselves a pastor?

2. Do you view other churches as competition or the body of Christ?

3.   How do you plan on discipling leaders who will also disciple?

4.   Are there particular denominations you are uncomfortable with viewing as followers of Jesus? Why?

Chapter 10: It's not time until...

Maybe you know all that you've read so far, and maybe you don't, but in this final chapter, I wanted to share with you when you're ready to start a home church. You see, I believe a time is coming when home churches in America will not only be an interesting sidebar to church life. People are becoming more and more hostile to Christianity than ever before. The reason for this is because of the power the American institutional church wields in our culture. American evangelicalism is a big part of American culture. For the last 100 years or so, Christians in America have shaped politics, entertainment, education, and several other branches of culture, and there will be backlash on some of the ways evangelicals abused their power and influence.

If we see that backlash, which some call persecution, the home church will become the predominant means by which the church gathers once again. I do want to make it clear that by persecution I don't mean trivial things like the church is no longer tax exempt if a pastor decides he can say hateful things from stage. I'm referring to the state or any other large branch of culture lashing out at the church for emphasizing that Jesus is Lord and emotionally or physically abusing anyone who believes and speaks that message.

When that time comes, the home church must be prepared to gather and be the church it was called to be as much as it may have been at the heights of 80's and 90's evangelicalism.

With all that in mind, I implore you to not start a home church unless the Spirit of God moves you to do so. You may have noticed that several of the chapters' steps involved prayer and that is no coincidence. Prayer invites God to speak to us and to move in us as we connect with the world at large.

In our technology savvy world, we have turned our backs on surrendering ourselves to His will, and chosen instead to do whatever we want to do. Like the Christian college student breaking up with our current date, we conveniently talk about God's will being whatever decision we have already made.

When God calls you to start a home church, then go after it with all of your might, like you would any venture, while remembering that the people in every church - home or institutional - who have surrendered their hearts to Christ, are His church. Your attitude on this topic, as a front runner of a launched home church, will help shape future Christian thought for those coming behind you.

Once you make a decision, and focus on unity in the body, ask God to bring like-minded, spirit-filled believers to partner with you in starting a home church. In our age of *nones* and people leaving the church in droves, there are a ton of people out there who want to obey Hebrews 10:24,25, but who have walked away from the church as an organization.

Once you find a person or a couple or a family, then start it up. You don't have to have eight plus people to have church. You only need more than one person who are willing to connect, pray together, read and study, take care of one another's needs, and be a light in your community. Then meet together on a regular basis. Along the way pray that God adds to your numbers daily.

It is vital, however, to be walking in His Spirit as individuals and as a church. Call on one another to live, walk, and immerse yourselves in the Spirit of God as Paul called all the believers to do throughout his letters. When you do that, and put Him before your family, entertainment, and technology, it will surprise you how powerful He is, and the things He can and will do in your life.

By powerful things, however, I'm not referring just to physical things. Sometimes churches point to amazing facilities or the number of people attending a gathering and shout how incredible God is. If this were true, we could all just point to a World Cup soccer game or how many people watch Super Bowl commercials each year and express how Great God is as a result of those stats.

Years ago, I sat in a small group with about fifteen people, including a couple who happened to be new believers. My sister, Brooke, happened to be visiting that night. The topic of the conversation that night in Millbury, Massachusetts was on prayer. After the conversation, we prayed for friends or family in our lives who needed prayer. One of the new believers, Scott, asked if he could pray for someone close to him. I said yes and he prayed for a coworker of his at his job in Westborough, Massachusetts. For the record, Westborough is about 20 minutes west of Millbury. Scott said his coworker's life was falling apart because of sickness, financial problems, family drama, and a hundred other issues that burdened his friend. Our small group gathered together and prayed intensely for his hurting coworker.

After the group, my sister and I decided to drove back home and on the way, we stopped in at a Wendy's about twenty minutes east of Millbury in north Worcester, Massachusetts. We made it in the dining room as the staff were locking the door, but they graciously allowed us to come in and eat. The room sat empty except the staff and one lady who sat in the corner eating by herself.

My sister and I sat and talked about our evening at the group, and in the middle of our conversation, she stood up and walked across the room and began to talk to the lonely lady, which in turn caused me to sit lonely and tired from the long day. I waited for my sister to finish talking to the lady, which she eventually did.   Then they walked over and my sister introduced me to Susan, a familiar name because our mother's name is Susan too. Brooke asked me if she could borrow my car to spend a little time with her new friend the following day, which I obliged.

Brooke drove and spent some time with Susan the next morning, then brought her back to the church I worked at, and told me she wanted to become a Christian. Susan and I prayed together that day, and with tears in our eyes, we all hugged and prayed for Susan and the new life she had just found in Christ.

Brooke went home, and the next week, I was pleased to be able to share with my small group the awesome story of Susan and how she came to Christ the week before in a Wendy's after our gathering. As I told the story and shared the lady's name,

Scott looked at me like I had three heads. He asked me to repeat her name and to describe what she looked like. I gave him that information. Then he proceeded to tell me that the person my sister walked across the room and talked to, and spent time with, and introduced her to Christ, was the same lady who we had prayed for an hour before in our small group.

We all felt goose bumps as we understood the power we accessed when we called out to God last week.

Any believer has access to His power when they allow Him to work through them, and do not allow our natural selves to get in the way of His supernatural love and power for the world. Your church can access that power, if they don't get in the way. Your family can access that power, if they don't get in the way. You can access that power, if you don't get in the way.

When He calls you to start a home church, do it. Access that power. Put away anything that obstructs it and allow Him free rein in your church.

Questions for the journey

1. Do you believe we can access the power of the Spirit of God?

2. Share a time when you saw God's supernatural power in your own life?

3. Do you feel called to starting a home church? Or being a part of starting one? Why or why not?

Outro: Details

As you move along and begin to start your home church, there are specific details you'll have to consider once you decide to actually start. I thought I'd make a list of those. Feel free to send me some others that I've missed.

*Where will we meet?

*Who will attend?

*How will we ensure that people are committed to the church?

*Will we eat?

*What will be our primary methods of communication within the group?

*What will our curriculum be? The Bible, Bible studies, Christian book studies?

*What will we do with the kids?

*What course of action will be taken if someone doesn't show up after a few weeks?

*How will we ensure that people communicate throughout the week and not just on the day we decide to meet?

*How will we decide to split up and multiply?

*How are the leaders held accountable?

*Will we allow visitors?

* Under what circumstances will we allow cancellations?

*What are my intense positions on theology and the Bible that the rest of the group should know?

*Will the leaders be ordained?

*Who will baptize?

*Who will administer the Lord's supper?

*What will our services look like and who will organize them?

*How will we decide when a church starts a 'ministry'?

*How will we ensure that different age groups have their needs met?

Appendix: Pandemic maneuvering

Since I finished the manuscript of this short book, a lot has happened in the world. A pandemic ravaged throughout the world, and the church and everything else looks completely different from the way it did just a few short weeks ago. I thought I'd add to what I had already written by sharing what I know about technology. My present church of the last 6 months (not a home church) is a small, struggling church full of good people and great community. However, technology was not on their radar when I arrived, and there was enough things I needed to work on that I didn't get to updating technology right away. Now there is a worldwide pandemic happening and the church was not prepared to build community online when it started. I'd like to share with you some of the technologies I've used in an effort to build community and continue discipleship in the midst of this tremendous hardship.

Group Communication

Just like in any group of people, Christian or not, there must be a tool to send communication to the entire group. There's nothing more frustrating than one or two people that are out of the loop, but the truth is there will always be people like that.

The trick is to communicate what tools you're using and share why you're using them.

Email - Old Faithful

Facebook Groups - Place your group in the setting that most of them are in anyways, and create a group around your home church.

Zoom - A fantastic videoconferencing app that allows as many people into your gathering as possible. Beware, however, that if you don't have the premium feature, Zoom limits you to a 40 minute time before it kicks you off. Ask people to become familiar with videoconferencing "etiquette".

Church online platform - Another amazing free tool from the people who gave us the Bible app and youversion.com. This is best for a teaching format. And others involved can "chat" through typing.

Planning Center - A great tool for institutional churches, but I have found it very convenient for smaller formats too, like home churches and groups.

Individual Communication

Group communication is important, but so is individually communicating with those whom you are discipling. As a home church, you could be living in a world where you actually can't meet with people in person. So how do you connect? How do you pour into the lives of others?

Phone - It's almost too easy, but since the late 1800's...

Face time - You may not like it, but video phone is upon us, and for anyone with an iPhone, it's the best way to communicate this way.   It's easy, reliable, and if you're organized, it's a great way to transfer information one on one.

Zoom - See above.

Google Duo - For anyone who doesn't have an iPhone.

Bible study tools

Without the Bible, your home church is destined for failure. I don't believe in worshiping it, but I do believe, as mentioned before, in its authority.   Reading, studying, and sharing the Word of God is a must for any home church.   Here are some tools to help you along the journey.

youversion.com (The Bible app) - A fantastic tool for online Bible reading.

Blue Letter Bible - Bible versions, but also commentaries, podcasts, and Lexicons.

Logos Bible Software - I can't even describe how good this is for Bible study.

There are other technologies I won't get into now, but as one author wrote, "Every organization is now a startup." Churches around the world will be thinking about how to apply best practices into this new world we live in, and that should include your home church.   Be in prayer and connect with other churches and Christians on social media. Pray through the best decisions to make regarding when, or how to meet in person or online.

Also, please do not make decisions based on political party lines. Follow wholeheartedly after what the Spirit of God has for you and your home church. He is calling us out into spiritual waters, and we need to be ready to move at any moment, or stay put should that be His desire for our lives.